How to be sure

1 John

by Nathan Buttery

Series Editor: Tim Chester

How to be sure: the Good Book Guide to 1 John
© Nathan Buttery/The Good Book Company, 2006.

The Good Book Company
Tel: 0845-225-0880
Fax: 0845-225-0990
Email: admin@thegoodbook.co.uk
Internet: www.thegoodbook.co.uk

ISBN 1 904889 95 6
ISBN 13: 9781904889953

Printed in the UK by Tyndale Press

CONTENTS

Introduction: Good Book Guides

Every Bible-study group is different—yours may take place in a church building, in a home, in a cafe, on a train, over a leisurely mid-morning coffee or squashed into a 30-minute lunch break. Your group may include new Christians, mature Christians, non-Christians, students, business colleagues or teens. That's why we've designed these *Good Book Guides* to be flexible for use in many different situations.

Our aim in each session is to uncover the meaning of a passage, and see how it fits into the 'big picture' of the Bible. But that can never be the end. We also need to apply appropriately what we have discovered to our lives. Let's take a look at what is included:

⊕ **Talkabout:** most groups need to 'break the ice' at the beginning of a session, and here's the question that will do that. It's designed to get people talking around a subject that will be covered in the course of the Bible study.

⊥ **Investigate:** the Bible text for each session is broken up into manageable chunks, with questions that aim to help you understand what the passage is about. **The Leader's Guide** contains **guidance on questions**, and sometimes ☑ additional 'follow-up' questions.

☺ **Explore more (optional):** these questions will help you connect what you have learned to other parts of the Bible, so you can begin to understand how the Bible fits together as a whole.

→ **Apply:** As you go through a Bible study, you'll keep coming across **apply** sections. The first part has questions to get the group discussing what the Bible teaching means in practice for you and your church. The second part, ☺ **getting personal**, is an opportunity for you to think, plan and pray about the changes that you personally may need to make as a result of what you have discovered.

↑ **Pray:** We want to encourage prayer that is rooted in God's Word—in line with His concerns, purposes and promises. So each session ends with an opportunity to review the truths and challenges highlighted by the Bible study, and turn them into prayers of request and thanksgiving.

The **Leader's Guide** and introduction provide historical background information, explanations of the Bible texts for each session, ideas for **optional extra** activities, and guidance on how best to help people uncover the truths of God's Word.

Why study *How to be sure*?

Do you wish you could be more confident? Some people never seem to suffer a moment's doubt about anything, whereas you fret and agonise with constant uncertainty. OK, so you're a Christian, but doesn't that just mean there are more and bigger things to be unsure about? We can be unsure about the truth of the gospel message; about whether God will judge or punish us; about whether our forgiveness is secure; about how to continue in the Christian life; and about our guidance for the future.

And so many different 'Christian' voices speak to us on matters of eternal life and death. How can we be sure of the real truth about Jesus? How do we know for certain that we are saved? How can we tell if others are truly from God or not?

At a time when the first-century church had been invaded by false teachers, the apostle John knew that Christians who are not sure of God's truth can wander away, never to return. He wrote to help his 'dear children', not only to know the real truth, but to be confident of it.

If then, why not today? We all urgently need to hear and obey God's loving message in this letter of John's. This Good Book Guide will help us to continue in Christ, so that we may be discerning about the truth, confident in its meaning for our lives and unashamed when He returns.

1
1 John 1 v 1-10
THE HEART OF THE MATTER

⊕ talkabout

1. What pressures do Christians, preachers and church leaders face to change the Christian message today?

⊕ investigate

The apostle John wrote to a group in churches in what is modern-day Turkey. False teachers were saying that physical things were evil and spiritual things were good. This led to two dangerous errors:

- They could not believe that Jesus Christ was the Son of God. Instead they said that the human person, Jesus, was anointed by 'the Christ' at His baptism, but then left Him at the cross. Jesus was just an ordinary man who was inspired for part of His life.
- They believed they could live as they wanted because what they did with their bodies does not matter. A distinctive Christian lifestyle was irrelevant.

John insists on the real life and death of Jesus Christ – God in the flesh. And he says that sin matters, and how Christians live is equally important.

▶ Read 1 John 1 v 1-4

2. What is the message that John proclaims? Why do you think he expresses it in this way?

3. What does John say about the Word of life?

4. Why does John proclaim the Word of life?

⊡ **apply**

5. The act of God becoming human is called 'the incarnation'. Why is the testimony of the apostles about the incarnation so important?

• How can we defend the Bible's teaching on the incarnation?

⊡ **getting personal**

Do you think a literal incarnation is important? Do you think the historical facts of Jesus, the God-man, are worth fighting for? Are you *willing* to defend it when the identity of Jesus comes up in conversation?

Do you know the joy of fellowship with God? Do you want other people to share that joy?

⊕ investigate

❯ Read 1 John 1 v 5-10

6. 'God is light' (v 5) could mean many things. What does John mean (look at how darkness and light are used in the rest of the passage)?

7. What false claims does John tackle in verses 6-10?

8. How does John respond to these false claims?

9. How is it possible for God to be both faithful *and* just when He forgives sin?

⊡ getting personal

When are you most tempted to think that sin doesn't matter? What kind of sins do you think of as 'little sins'?

What confidence do you have that your future is secure with God? Is it based on a false confidence in your ability to clean up your life? Or is it a true confidence in the faithfulness of God, expressed in the death of Christ on the cross?

⊡ apply

John opposes people who do not take sin seriously. They think sin does not matter (v 6-7) or can easily be overcome (v 8-10).

10. How might a weak view of sin affect our spiritual lives?

11. Why is it important to keep the cross at the forefront of our lives?

⊡ pray

that God would help you

- to trust the message of the apostles about Jesus, the God-man;

- to delight in the God who is light, so that you want to walk in His light;

- to keep the cross at the forefront of your life.

Spend some time confessing your sin (either out loud or in silence). Close by using the words of verses 8-9.

2 1 John 2 v 1-14
WALKING THE TALK

⊕ talkabout

1. How can we know that someone is a true Christian?

⊕ investigate

> **Read 1 John 2 v 1-2**

2. What encouragement does John give for us when we sin?

In verse 2 John says Jesus is the 'propitiation' ('atoning sacrifice') for our sins. Propitiation means making God favourably disposed towards us by turning aside His wrath. God should judge us for our sin but, because of the cross, He gives us the blessing of forgiveness instead. Jesus did this by turning aside the wrath of God, which should have fallen on us, so that it fell on Him instead, on the cross. We must not think that Jesus persuaded or forced the Father to bless us through the cross, as if the Father was unwilling. Our salvation starts with the love of God. The cross was God's loving plan to be both just and to forgive our sins (1 v 9).

⊟ **apply**

3. How might you use these words to comfort a Christian friend who is worried about their sin and guilt?

4. Why do you think John adds 'not only for ours, but also for the sins of the whole world'?

⊡ **investigate**

> ❯ **Read 1 John 2 v 3-6**

5. How do these verses help us assess people who say: 'I know God'?

6.   What does it mean for God's love to be made complete in us?

▶ **Read 1 John 2 v 7-11**

7.   In what sense is the command to love one another an old command?

8.   In what sense is the command to love one another a new command?

9.   Why does John make hatred or love towards other Christians the test of true conversion?

▶ **Read 1 John 2 v 12-14**

John often addresses his readers as 'dear children' (2 v 1, 18, 28), so the 'dear children' are *all* Christians. The fathers are the older Christians, many of whom may also have seen Jesus when He lived on earth, as John did. The younger men are the new generation, who must take on the struggle to proclaim and live the truth.

10. Why does John write to his readers? What encouragement does he want to give to them?

⊡ **explore more**

In verses 12-14 John reiterates why he writes this letter. Look back over 1 v 1 – 2 v 11. Where else has John told us why he writes? How do these explanations link to verses 12-14?

⊡ **apply**

11. How might you use verses 3-11 to challenge a Christian friend who is complacent about sin in their life?

12. How might hatred towards another Christian show itself?

getting personal

John is speaking to two different sorts of people:

- **the fearful**, who think that because they sin, they cannot truly know God;

- **the complacent,** who think that because God forgives them, it does not matter how they live.

Which is the greatest danger you face – complacency or fear? How do these verses help you avoid that danger?

pray

Use verses 1-2 to pray for people who are worried about their sin.

Use verses 3-6 to pray for people who are complacent about their sin.

Use verses 7-11 to pray that your group might live in the light by loving one another.

3

STAYING THE COURSE

⊕ talkabout

1. What do you think is the main failing of British churches? What is the main failing of your congregation?

⊕ investigate

> **Read 1 John 2 v 15-17**

2 What does John mean when he tells us not to love the world?

3. Look at verse 16. How does John describe the actions and attitudes of the world?

⊕ apply

4. Identify some examples of these actions and attitudes that you see today?

5. Where can you see signs of worldliness in your life or the life of your church?

⬇ investigate

6. Why is love for the world so destructive for the Christian?

▣ getting personal

Think about the things which influence you away from walking with God. They might include the attitudes of your culture, the opinions of your friends, the particular temptations of your life. What can you do to reduce their influence? What can you do to counter their influence?

⬇ investigate

❯ Read 1 John 2 v 18-27

The Bible teaches that a 'man of lawlessness' will arise at the end of time (2 Thessalonians 2). This figure will provide a focus for opposition to God and His people. John calls him 'the antichrist'— the opposite and opponent of Christ. But John also says we are already living in the last hour (v 18) and already antichrists have come—people who oppose Christ by denying the truth.

⊡ explore more

Read 2 Thessalonians 2 v 1-17. What does Paul says about 'the man of lawlessness'? How does he say Christians should respond to this teaching? How should we pray for one another?

⊡ investigate

7. What are the marks of antichrists?

8. Why are the antichrists so dangerous?

The word 'Christ' means 'anointed One'. Jesus, the true Christ, is God's anointed King and Saviour. Antichrists have a false anointing that denies the truth. John says believers also have an anointing from God. We are 'anointed ones' (= Christ-ians).

9. What is the result of our anointing?

10. Why does John say we do not need anyone to teach us? Does this mean we do not need Bible teachers in the church?

⊡ apply

11. Where do we see these things happening today?

12. Look at v 24-25. What does it mean in practice to 'remain in the truth'?

⤴ **pray**

In 2 Thessalonians 2 Paul describes a coming man of lawlessness. He ends his description of his coming with a prayer in verses 16-17.

Use this to pray for one another as you live in an anti-Christian world:

> *'May our Lord Jesus Christ Himself and God our Father, who loved us and by his grace gave us eternal encouragement and good hope, encourage our hearts and strengthen us in every good deed and word.'*

1 John 2 v 28 – 3 v 10

4 FAMILY LIKENESS

⊕ talkabout

1. How are you like your parents? In what ways are you becoming more like your parents as you grow older?

⊕ investigate

▶ **Read 1 John 2 v 28-29**

2. What gives us confidence for the future?

3. Does doing what is right give us confidence before God?

▶ Read 1 John 3 v 1-3

4. Look at verse 1. How does John feel as he writes these words? Why does he feel this way?

5. What are the results of becoming a child of God?

⊡ apply

6. What practical difference does it make to remember that you are a child of God?

7. What practical difference does it make to remember that you will share God's glory?

⊡ getting personal

Make a list of words that describe God: loving, holy, merciful and so on. We are to be like our Father. Look at the list. How do you measure up?

⊕ investigate

▶ Read 1 John 3 v 4-10

8. Look at v 4. How does John's description of sin motivate us to stop sinning?

9. Look at verses 5-6. What reason does John give for us to stop sinning?

10. What encouragement does John give us in these verses?

11. What does John mean when he says Christians no longer sin (v 6 and 9)?

⊡ getting personal

▶ Read Galatians 5 v 16-17.
Try to think of times in your experience when you have felt the conflict between the Spirit within you and your sinful nature.

⬇ **investigate**

12. Look at verses 7-10. What reason does John give for us to stop sinning?

13. What encouragement does John give us in these verses?

➡ **apply**

14. How would you use these verses to challenge someone who claimed to be a Christian, but was unconcerned about sin in their life?

15. How would you use these verses to respond to someone who wants to know how they can stop sinning?

⬆ **pray**

'How great is the love the Father has lavished on us, that we should be called children of God! And that is what we are! The reason the world does not know us is that it did not know him.' (v 1)

John is amazed at God's lavish love in taking His enemies and making them His children. **Use Romans 8 v 15-17** and **Galatians 4 v 1-7** to praise God for the privileges of being His children.

5 1 John 3 v 10-24
FAMILY TIES

⊕ **talkabout**

1. Love is ... What are some of the ways the world around us completes this sentence?

⊕ **investigate**

In 3 v 1-10 John said that we show we are God's children by living in obedience to God. Now he argues that we show we are God's children by loving our fellow brothers and sisters.

▶ **Read 1 John 3 v 10-15**

2. How do the children of the devil behave?

3. Why does John chose Cain as an example?

4. How do the children of God behave?

5. How do the children of the devil treat the children of God?

❯ Read 1 John 3 v 16-18

6. How does John define love? How does this definition compare to your answers to question 1?

⊡ apply

In verses 17-18 John says that love cannot remain theoretical. It must be expressed in practical ways.

7. How do we sometimes 'love with words' without action?

8. How can you put this true love into practice in your situation?

⊻ investigate

> ❯ Read 1 John 3 v 19-20

9. How can our hearts condemn us?

10. How can we set our hearts at rest? What two remedies does this passage suggest we apply to our feelings of guilt?

> ❯ Read 1 John 3 v 21-24

11. What is the link between v 19-20 and v 21?

12. John says God will give us anything we ask. What stops this becoming self-indulgent?

⊡ getting personal

Do you struggle with a sense of guilt when you approach God in prayer, when reading the Bible, or in public worship? How can this passage comfort you?

⊡ apply

13. How should we pray?

⊡ pray

Use verses 23-24 as the basis for your prayers for one another. Pray for:

- more faith in Jesus;

- more love for other Christians;

- more obedience to God.

1 John 4 v 1-21
TRUE LOVE

⊕ talkabout

1. How does our culture define a 'spiritual' person?

⊥ investigate

Plenty of people in John's day claimed to be spiritual or spirit-inspired. But John warns his readers not to be gullible.

▶ Read 1 John 4 v 1-6

2. Why do Christians need to be discerning?

3. What is the test that it is the Spirit of God who is at work?

4. What comfort does John give us when we feel overwhelmed or perplexed by false claims?

⊡ apply

5. People often claim there is a renewed interest in spirituality in our society. How should we assess this?

6. The test of spirituality or claims to be Spirit-inspired is how people view the identity and work of Jesus. For John, the test was whether people believed Jesus was truly human. What are the issues today? Where do we see false claims about Jesus? Where do we see false spiritualities?

⊡ investigate

▶ Read 1 John 4 v 7-21

7. Look at verses 7-12. Why should we love one another?

8. How should we love one another?

9. Look at verses 13-16. How can we know that we are Christians?

Is love for others or belief in the truth the most important sign that someone follows correct teaching? What is John's definition of love in v 9? What is John's definition of truth in v 14?

⊡ investigate

10. Look at verses 17-18. What is the goal or completion of love?

11. The Bible tells us to fear God. So what does John mean when he says 'perfect love drives out fear'?

12. How does verse 19 give us confidence?

⊡ apply

13. Look at v 12. The invisible God is, in some sense, made visible through our love. What are the implications of this for:

- evangelism?

- pastoral care?

14. Identify one thing you have learnt about love from these verses.

• Identify one thing you will do as a result of studying these verses.

⊡ **getting personal**

According to John, true Christians:

- have received the Spirit (v 13);

- believe the truth about Jesus (v 14-15);

- love one another (v 16).

These signs are not a checklist, but three confirmations that work together. Are you a true Christian? Are you a confident Christian?

⊕ **pray**

• Give thanks to God for His love to us and the confidence it gives us.

• Ask God to help you love your brothers and sisters—especially those who you find difficult to love.

• Pray that the love of your church will commend the gospel to unbelievers.

7

1 John 5 v 1-21

TRUE CONFIDENCE

⊕ talkabout

1. Where do people look to find confidence?

⊕ investigate

John wants his readers to have confidence and assurance. This has been the aim of the whole letter and, as he concludes, he brings all his themes together.

❯ Read 1 John 5 v 1-5

2. See if you can identify the connections in these verses.
What is the cause of what?

3. What does it mean to overcome the world? (See also 2 v 15-17.)

❯ Read 1 John 5 v 6-12

The false teachers denied that Jesus had come in the flesh (4 v 2). They probably claimed that divine qualities came on Jesus at His baptism and left at the cross. But John says Jesus came 'through' (ESV) water and blood. He was divine before, during and after His baptism and the cross. He was God all the time.

4. How do the Spirit, the water and the blood testify about Jesus (v 7-8)?

5. What does John mean when he says 'we accept man's testimony' (v 9)?

6. What does John mean by God's testimony (v 9)?

7. Why does 'theology' matter so much?

❯ Read 1 John 5 v 13-17

8. John writes this letter so that we know that we have eternal life (v 13). Look back over the letter and identify the 'tests' that reveal a true Christian.

Assurance that we are children of God leads to assurance that we can approach our heavenly Father in prayer.

9. What does it mean to pray according to God's will (v 14)?

⊡ **explore more**

Look back over 1 John. What does John say is God's will for our lives? What promises from God does John give? How could we turn these into prayer?

⊡ **investigate**

10. How should we pray for believers who fall into sin?

> **Read 1 John 5 v 18-21**

11. What does John say we 'know' in these verses?

12. How should this knowledge affect our lives?

13. Why do you think John ends with a call to keep ourselves from idols (v 21)?

⊡ apply

14. How would you use 1 John with the following people?

- someone who doubts they are a Christian because of the guilt they feel about some past sin

- someone who thinks they are a Christian, but has no concern to love others

- someone who doubts they are a Christian and, when you probe further, admits with shame that they're having an affair

⊡ pray

As you finish your studies in 1 John, share together:

- one truth you have learnt or seen afresh;

- one thing that you have decided to do as a result.

Praise God for the truths you have learnt and ask God for help to do the actions you have identified.

How to be sure
1 John
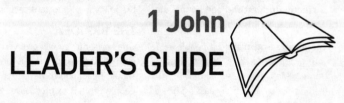
LEADER'S GUIDE

How to be sure: Leader's Guide

Introduction

Leading a Bible study can be a bit like herding cats—everyone has a different idea of what the passage could be about, and a different line of enquiry that they want to pursue. But a good group leader is more than someone who just referees this kind of discussion. You will want to:

- **correctly understand** and handle the Bible passage. But also…

- **encourage and train** the people in your group to do this for themselves. Don't fall into the trap of spoon-feeding people by simply passing on the information in the Leader's Guide. Then…

- make sure that no Bible study is finished without everyone knowing how the passage is **relevant** for them. What changes do you all need to make in the light of the things you have been learning? And finally…

- encourage the group to turn all that has been learned and discussed into **prayer.**

Your Bible-study group is unique, and you are likely to know better than anyone the capabilities, backgrounds and circumstances of the people you are leading. That's why we've designed these guides with a number of optional features. If they're a quiet bunch, you might want to spend longer on **talkabout**. If your time is limited you can choose to skip **explore more**, or get people to look at these questions at home. As leader, you can adapt and select the material to the needs of your particular group.

So what's in the Leader's Guide?

The main thing that this Leader's Guide will help you to do is to understand the major teaching points in the passage you are studying, and how to apply them. As well as guidance on the questions, the Leader's Guide for each session contains the following important sections:

THE BIG IDEA

One key sentence will give you the main point of the session. This is what you should be aiming to have fixed in people's minds as they leave the Bible study. And it's the point you need to head back towards when the discussion goes off at a tangent.

SUMMARY

An overview of the passage, including plenty of useful historical background information.

OPTIONAL EXTRA

Usually this is an introductory activity, that ties in with the main theme of the Bible study, and is designed to 'break the ice' at the beginning of a session. Or it may be a 'homework project' that people can tackle during the week.

So let's take a look at the various features of a Good Book Guide.

⊕ **talkabout**: each session kicks off with a discussion question, based on the group's opinions or experiences. It's designed to get people talking and thinking in a general way about the main subject of the Bible study.

⊥ **investigate**: the first thing that you and your group need to know is what the Bible passage is about, which is the purpose of these questions. But watch out—people may come up with answers based on their experiences or teaching they have heard in the past, without referring to the passage at all. It's amazing how often we can get through a Bible study without actually looking at the Bible! If you're stuck for an answer the Leader's Guide contains guidance on questions. These are the answers to which you need to direct your group. This information isn't meant to be read out to people—ideally, you want them to discover these answers from the Bible for themselves. Sometimes optional follow-up questions (see ⊗ in guidance on questions) are included, to help you help your group get to the answer.

⊙ **explore more**: these questions generally point people to other relevant parts of the Bible. They are useful for helping your group to see how the passage fits into the 'big picture' of the whole Bible. These sections are **OPTIONAL**—only use them if you have time. Remember—it's better to finish in good time having really grasped one big thing from the passage, than to try and cram everything in.

⊖ **apply**: we want to encourage you to spend more time working at application—too often, it is simply tacked on at the end. In the **Good Book Guides**, apply sections are mixed in with the investigate sections of the study. We hope that people will realise that application is not just an optional extra, but rather, the whole purpose of studying the Bible. We do Bible study so

that our lives can be changed by what we hear from God's Word. If you skip the application, the Bible study hasn't achieved its purpose.

These questions draw out practical lessons that we can all learn from the Bible passage. You can review what has been learned so far, and think about practical differences that this should make in our churches and our lives. The group gets the opportunity to talk about what they personally have learned.

⊡ **getting personal**, can be done at home, or you could allocate a few moments of quiet reflection for each person to think about specific changes that they need to make and pray through in their own lives.

Why not have a time for reporting back at the beginning of the following session, so that everyone can be encouraged and challenged by one another to make application a priority?

⬆ **pray**: In Acts 4 v 25-30 the first Christians quoted Psalm 2 as they prayed in response to the persecution of the apostles by the Jewish religious leaders. Today however, it's not as common for Christians to base prayers on the truths of God's Word as it once was. As a result, our prayers tend to be weak, superficial and self-centred rather than bold, visionary and God-centred. The prayer section is based on what has been learned from the Bible passage. How different our prayer times would be if we were genuinely responding to what God has said to us through His Word.

1 John 1 v 1-10

THE HEART OF THE MATTER

THE BIG IDEA
We can enjoy fellowship with God because Jesus is the God-man who reconciles us to God by dying for our sin.

SUMMARY
John begins by affirming the truth of the incarnation. The incarnation is the act of God becoming human. The eternal Word, which was from the beginning, became flesh. Jesus is both truly God and truly human. John can affirm this truth because he and the other apostles ('we') saw, touched and heard Jesus for themselves. The historical facts of the incarnation matter because Jesus the God-man restores our connection with God so that we can enjoy fellowship with God. John wants his readers to share with him the joy of knowing God.

John then tackles two false claims that prevent us enjoying fellowship with God:

• I can know God and still walk in darkness (v 6-7)

• I can know God because I am without sin (v 8-10)

John says these are both lies. Light and darkness do not mix. To know God is to want to please God (= not walking in darkness). We do continue to sin. But Jesus purifies us from sin and God forgives us our sin.

GUIDANCE ON QUESTIONS
1.

• Which particular Christian truths are unpopular today?
• Have you yourself faced pressures to change the Christian message?

2. Verses 1-4 are all one sentence in the original Greek with the main verb 'we proclaim' (v 1). John proclaims the Word of life, which was from the beginning.

3. John says the Word appeared as a person who could be seen, touched and heard.

• What personal claims does John make? John claims that he himself saw, touched and heard the Word of life.

4.

• What is the fellowship in which John rejoices? Knowing the Father and his Son, Jesus. John proclaims the Word so that we might share this fellowship with the Father and the Son. John wants us to have fellowship with him in having fellowship with God. Fellowship = community, union, knowing, relationship.

5. APPLY: John emphasises that he and the other apostles ('we') saw, touched and heard the Word of life. He emphasises the historical truth of the incarnation. Sometimes people have said Jesus was God, but not truly human (this was the situation John faced). Sometimes people have said Jesus was human, but not truly God (this is more common today). But Jesus is truly God and truly human. Only Jesus the God-man can connect human beings in fellowship to God (see 1 Timothy 2 v 5). Only Jesus can make our joy complete.

The following suggestions may be helpful for Christians defending the Bible's teaching on the incarnation:

- Make sure that you know **the evidence for the truth of the incarnation**—the aspects of Jesus' life that demonstrate his human nature; the miracles, claims and character of Jesus that point to His divine nature; the details and agreement of the Gospel accounts that show the disciples to be eye-witnesses and conscientious recorders of historical facts.
- Thing about **the way you talk** about Jesus and the impression you give. Does it sound like myth or historical fact? Avoid phrases such as 'I think...' or 'As a Christian, I believe...'. Use phrases like: 'The Gospel writers mention...' or 'The Bible records...'.
- Most importantly, encourage people to read about Jesus in the Gospels to decide for themselves whether Jesus is myth or historical fact. Give them a Gospel, or a recording of a Gospel. Or offer to read through a Gospel with them.
- Keep returning to the point of Jesus' mission, and the question of how God could justly forgive sins if Jesus was either not God, or not human.

6. In the Bible, light is a picture of both revelation and goodness. God is light because He reveals the truth (v 6); God is light because He is perfect and pure.

How do we use light and dark in the same way in our culture today?
'Being in the dark' = not knowing what is going on. 'The light went on in my head' = I understood. 'It is a dark place' = it is a morally bad place. 'She lights up the room' = she brings joy.

7 and 8.

	False claim	John's response
v 6-7	I can know God and still walk in darkness. Sin does not matter.	This is a lie. Light and darkness do not mix. Switch on the light and the darkness is dispelled. We walk in the light (= living to please God) and depend on the cross to purify us from the sins we continue to commit.
v 8-10	I can know God because I am without sin. I do not sin any more.	This is also a lie. I am a sinner and I do sin. Not only is this a lie, but it portrays God as liar since it contradicts what He says in His word (v 10). Even though I sin, I can know God because God forgives me.

9. God is faithful to His promises and His covenant. **See Matthew 26 v 27-28.** We can be confident God will forgive us when we confess our sin to Him, because He has promised to forgive those who trust in Jesus. God is just when He forgives, because Jesus took the punishment we deserve on the cross. God does not simply ignore sin. He justly punishes our sin, but that punishment falls on Jesus instead of us. Our forgiveness is for real.

EXPLORE MORE

Both openings speak of the Word which was from the beginning becoming flesh so that He could be seen and touched. The Word is the Word of life that brings life. Both passages speak of light and darkness. Jesus brought the light of God into the world, but some people continue to walk in darkness. John's Gospel says we become children of God by *receiving* the Word, while 1 John says we have fellowship with God *through* the Word.

10. APPLY: A weak view of sin is a lie (v 6, 8, 10) and we cannot live a lie. If we think sin does not matter, then we cannot enjoy fellowship with God (v 6). We will not keep fighting temptation or turning from sin in repentance. Above all, a weak view of sin leads to a weak view of the cross (v 7, 9) and therefore, of God's covenant faithfulness and justice.

• How does a weak view of sin affect the way we think about the cross?

11. APPLY: The cross reminds us of our sin (our sin was so great that only the death of God's Son could remedy it). The cross reminds us of God's purity (God could not have fellowship with us without dealing with our sin). The cross reminds us of God's forgiveness (and that gives us a new identity and a new lifestyle). The cross reminds us of God's faithfulness and justice (we can rely on God's forgiveness because it rests on His covenant promises and is consistent with His justice).

OPTIONAL EXTRA

At the beginning of the session, ask people to skim read 1 John looking for repeated or common words. You could give people a printout or photocopy of the letter so that they can mark repeated words. What does this survey suggest are key concerns for John as he writes this letter?

1 John 2 v 1-14
WALKING THE TALK

THE BIG IDEA
A true Christian is someone with faith in Jesus that makes a difference to their lives.

SUMMARY
John writes so that we will not sin. But he recognises that all of us do continue to sin. So he comforts us by reminding us that Jesus is our advocate before the Father. Jesus defends us, not by arguing we are innocent (we are not – 1 v 8); instead, Jesus took our sin and punishment on Himself. He died as an atoning sacrifice for our sins.

John not only comforts those who are worried about their sin. He also challenges those who are complacent about their sin. If we know God, then we will want to please Him by obeying His commands and becoming more like Jesus. If we are not interested in pleasing God, then we cannot claim to know Him or love Him.

The focal point of God's commands is the command to love one another. This old command has been given a new context. Love is the characteristic of the coming age of light that dawned with the first coming of Jesus. Hatred is the characteristic of the old age of darkness that is passing away. Those who continue to hate other people are part of this old age of darkness.

Verses 12-14 summarise what John has been saying so far. We can know the Father because the Word (Jesus) has appeared in the flesh to reconcile us to God. As a result, we are part of the coming age of love and light. We have overcome the old, dark age and the reign of the evil one (Satan).

GUIDANCE ON QUESTIONS
1.

> What are the signs should we look for in a true Christian?

There is no need to 'correct' different opinions at this stage. The study as a whole will answer this question. But you may want to highlight any difference of opinion between those who think it is what people *say* they believe, and those who think it is what people *do*. John argues in these verses that there is an inevitable link between what we believe and what we do. A true Christian is someone with faith in Jesus that makes a difference to their lives.

Note: This question is not about what *makes* someone a true Christian, but how other people *can know* someone is a true Christian.

2. John points us to the work of Christ. John uses the imagery of a courtroom. We are in the dock, but Jesus is our advocate (v 1). Jesus speaks to the Father on our behalf – not because we are innocent, but because He has already taken our punishment. He sacrificed Himself in our place on the cross (v 2).

3. APPLY: Encourage people to express the ideas in verses 1-2 in simple, contemporary language.

4. APPLY: There is a danger that we will sit back and enjoy our forgiveness without sharing God's concern for the world. We can become insular, living within our comfort zone instead of boldly proclaiming the cross to a needy world. John's joy is complete as other people share his fellowship with God (1 v 3-4).

• **What happens when we forget God's concern for the world?**

5. The claim 'I know God' is true if we want to obey God (v 3). The claim 'I know God' is false if we do not want to obey God (v 4). We show that we know and love God by wanting to obey and please Him.

• **How would you assess the claim 'I love my wife (or husband)?' What are the parallels with the claim 'I know God'?**

6. It does not mean God's love is lacking in some way without us. It means God's love achieve its purpose in our lives.

• **What is the purpose of God's love?** See verse 6. That we might be like Jesus (see Romans 8 v 28-29). Obeying God = living like Jesus.

7. John imagines someone responding. 'Hang on a minute. When I signed up to Christianity I was told it was all about grace and mercy. It wasn't what I did that counted, but what God had done from me. Now you're springing something new on me, telling me that what I do matters after all.' John says love has always been part of the Christian message. See also Leviticus 19 v 18.

8. John gives two reasons. First, 'its truth is seen in him and you'. See John 13 v 34-35. Jesus redefines or gives new content to the meaning of love. Second, 'because the darkness is passing and the true life is already shining.' Love is the characteristic of the new age of God's kingdom, which began with the first coming of King Jesus and will be completed when He returns. In the meantime, we live in a twilight zone—the darkness of Satan's rule is fading, while the daylight of God's rule has begun to dawn.

9. Hatred is the characteristic of the passing age of darkness (v 9, 11). Love is the characteristic of the coming age of light (v 10). Our hatred or love reveals our allegiance.

10. John wants his readers to be sure of the following:
• that although they are sinners, they have been forgiven in Christ (2 v 12);
• that when they know Jesus, they know God (2 v 13-14)—this is because Jesus is the God-man;
• that they are on the side that has already won (2 v 13-14).

• How do these encouragements link with what John has already written? (see the Explore More section below.) This is an opportunity to review Sessions 1 and 2.

EXPLORE MORE

See 2 v 1. In 1 v 5 – 2 v 2 John says that, though we are sinners, we can know God because God forgives us. This is why John writes to 'you, dear children'. 'Children' is what John calls all his readers – ie: all Christians (eg: 2 v 18).

See 1 v 4. In 1 v 1-4 John says that the Word was truly seen and known in human form. This is why John writes to 'you, fathers'. The fathers are those older men who also saw Jesus during His time on earth.

See 2 v 7–8. In 2 v 3-11 John tells his readers to love one another because love is the characteristic of the new age of light, which is overcoming the dark reign of the evil one. This is why John writes to 'you, young men'. A new generation must take up the struggle to live and proclaim the truth.

11. APPLY: A true Christian is someone with faith in Jesus that makes a difference to their lives. If our faith does not make a difference, then we cannot be sure we are a true Christian.

12. APPLY: Christians are rarely openly antagonistic or nasty towards others. But signs of hatred are avoidance, bitterness, conflict and lack of concern. Hatred is the absence of love. We hate when we do not love.

• How can we counter hatred in our hearts? By remembering all that God has done to us and the forgiveness that he shows for our faults.

3

1 John 2 v 15-27

STAYING THE COURSE

THE BIG IDEA

We are to continue trusting in Jesus, in the face of the temptations of the world around us and people who deny the truth or claim special insight.

SUMMARY

In this section John contrasts:
• the world and the Christian (v 15-17)
• the antichrists and the Christian (v 18-27)

John sometimes uses the word 'world' to describe the created order, including human beings, which God loves. But here he uses it to refer to human society and culture in opposition to God. It refers to the influences in our culture and among our friends that move us away from God.

The Bible describes a 'man of lawlessness' who will set himself up at the end to be worshipped in opposition to God (2

Thessalonians 2). John calls him 'the antichrist'—the opposite and opponent of Christ. But John also says antichrists have already come. They are people who oppose Christ, by denying the truth or claiming special insight. The word 'Christ' means 'anointed one'. Jesus Christ is God's true anointed one. Antichrists have a false anointing. But John says believers also have an anointing from God (we are Christ-ians). Our anointing enables us to know the truth that was from the beginning—that Jesus is the true Christ and the Son of God.

We are to remain *in the truth* (= to keep believing in Jesus) in an anti-Christian world.

GUIDANCE ON QUESTIONS

1. Try to avoid a moaning session! Steer people away from criticisms of church leaders (especially the leaders of your church) or other specific individuals. Ask them to think about the congregation as a whole.

2. You may want to point people to John 3 v 16, where Jesus tells us that God Himself loves the world. How do we reconcile these two statements? John uses the word 'world' in two different ways. First, it refers to the created universe including people. God loves what He has made and sent Jesus to save us. Secondly, the word 'world' refers to human society and culture in opposition to God. It is the world in this second sense that we are not to love. We are to avoid anything that pulls us away from God (see Psalm 1).

3. John talks about 'the cravings of sinful man, the lust of his eyes and the

boasting of what he has and does.' Ask people to express these in their own words.

- **the craving of sinful man** = the pressure to sin from within ourselves because of our sinful desires
- **the lust of his eyes** = the pressure to sin from outside when we see something that we desire – a wrong desire or a desire that is greater than our desire for God
- **the boasting in what he has or does** = the pressure to sin from a world that justifies or celebrates sin.

4. APPLY: This is an opportunity for people to link God's Word with their own experience and observations.

5. APPLY: Remind people of John's definition of worldliness in v 16 as you discuss this question.

6. See verse 17.

EXPLORE MORE

The man of lawlessness will set himself up to be worshipped in the place of God (v 4). He will perform amazing signs (v 9). The spirit of lawlessness or opposition to God is already at work in the world, but at present God restrains it (v 6-7). And one day Jesus will destroy all opposition to God (v 8). Some people think the man of lawlessness is a specific future person; other people that it is a picture of opposition to God in any and every age (eg: communist regimes). Paul describes how we should respond in verses 13-15 and how we should pray in verses 16-17.

7. The antichrists that John describes are people who have been part of the church, but who have now left (v 19).

They deny that Jesus is the Christ and God's divine Son (v 22). It is also likely that the antichrists claimed special knowledge or insight that 'ordinary' Christians did not have (v 21, 27).

8. See verse 26. The antichrists threaten to lead Christians astray.

9. Look at v 21. We all know the truth. Look at v 27. We do not need teachers because we know all things.

10. It seems the antichrists claimed special knowledge that 'ordinary' Christians did not have (v 21, 27). They claimed to have access to secret knowledge. But John says the Word of life has been seen and heard (1 v 1-2). God's revelation is not secret. It is openly proclaimed (1 v 3). We do not need special teachers to bring God's truth to us. The truth is there for all to see in the testimony of the apostles (and now in the Bible), and the Holy Spirit helps us understand it. This is the truth that has been heard from the beginning (v 24 and 1 v 1). True Bible teachers help us understand what God has *already said* in His Word. So we do not need people to tell us what God is saying.

11. Where do we see people who have left the church? Where do we see people who deny the truth about Jesus? Where do we see people who claim special knowledge or insight that ordinary believers do not have?

12. Remaining in the truth means to continue to believe that Jesus is the Christ and the Son of God (v 22-23). The antichrists did not remain (v 19) because they denied this truth (v 22).

John talks about 'remaining' in v 19, 24, 27.
• **Summarise what John says about remaining and not remaining.**
• **What can we do to encourage one another to remain in the truth?**
Talk about the role of regular Bible reading, prayer, worship and Christian community in helping us remain in the truth.

OPTIONAL EXTRA

Bring some Sunday supplements and other magazines. Ask people to flick through, looking at the articles and adverts. How do they encourage us to think in un-Christian ways? How do they encourage us to live in un-Christian ways? How do they encourage sinful cravings and lusts? Discuss how people are influenced by these things.

1 John 2 v 28 – 3 v 10

FAMILY LIKENESS

THE BIG IDEA

In a great act of love, God has made us His children and so now we should behave as His children.

SUMMARY

John says we can be confident for the future if we continue in Him (= remaining in the truth or believing in Jesus; 2 v 22-24). It is not that continuing in Jesus itself saves us. It is, rather, a sign that we have been born of God. Since God is righteous, those who are born of God will behave in a righteous way (= do what is right v 29).

In a wonderful act of love, God has made us His children (v 1). The world hates us because they are not part of God's family (v 1). One day we will become like God (v 2), and that should motivate us to live like God now (v 3).

Jesus came to take away sin, and so we should stop sinning (v 4-6). We are part of God's family and so we show the family likeness by not sinning (v 7, 9). If we continue to sin without trying to stop, we show that we belong to another family—the family of Satan (v 8, 10).

In the New Testament Christians are often told:

- **to be what we are:** we are children of God so we should show the family likeness;

- **to become what we *will be*:** we will be like God in the new creation, so we should be like Him now.

GUIDANCE ON QUESTIONS

1. Encourage people to include both similarities in appearance and character.

• **How are your children like you?** If the group knows one another's families, you could encourage them to identify similarities in other families.

2. We can have confidence when we continue in Christ.

• **What does it mean to 'continue in Christ'.** See 2 v 22-25. It means to remain in Christ by believing the truth that He is God's Son and God's anointed Saviour-King.

3. Yes and no! We are not saved because we do what is right (salvation by works). But doing what is right can give us confidence. It is a sign that we have been born of God. God's gift of new birth makes us right in His sight. But it also changes the way we live. Since God is righteous, those who are born of God will behave in a righteous way.

4. As we read verse 1, we can sense John's amazement and excitement. God has taken His enemies and made them His children.

5. The world will be hostile towards us (v 1). Imagine how people would react to you if you were adopted by a notorious hate figure. One day we will live with our Father in glory and we will become like Him (v 2). Change is certain for the Christian. In the meantime, we try to behave like our Father (v 3).

6. APPLY: You may want to create some scenarios of people facing temptation and ask what difference being a child of God makes in each situation.

7. APPLY: See Matthew 6 v 19-21 and Colossians 3 v 1-5.

8.

• Whose law is it that we break?

Sin is an act of rebellion against God. And for the Christian, God is not a distant, authoritarian law-maker, but the Father, who has lavished His love on us.

9. Jesus came to take away our sins. God has saved us so that we can stop sinning.

10. Jesus came to take away sin. The guilt of sin is forgiven and the power of sin is broken. We are free to live as God's children.

11. John does not mean Christians cannot sin. See 1 v 8. He talks about people who keep on sinning. If we keep on sinning without trying to stop, then we probably do not know Christ. Sinning is now unacceptable for Christians. Sadly, we do still sin, but true Christians always struggle against sin. Every Christian sins, but a true Christian cannot go on sinning without being concerned and without struggling to put it right.

12. Refer people back to question 1. Our character reveals the family to which we belong. If we are part of God's family, we will show the family likeness by not sinning (v 7, 9). If we continue to sin without trying to stop, we show that we belong to the family of Satan (v 8, 10).

13. We were born with a bias towards sin. Now we have been born again of God with a bias *away* from sin. We have God's seed in us—holiness is in our DNA.

14. APPLY: We are not saved by our righteous acts. But doing what is right is a sign that we are children of the righteous One (2 v 29; 3 v 7, 9). Sinning is a sign that we are children of Satan (3 v 8, 10).

15. APPLY: The first step to overcoming sin is to be born of God by faith. We need to constantly remind ourselves of our new identity in Christ. We are children of God. This is both the basis and motivation for change in our lives. Compared with what sin offers, we have something much better—God's lavish love and the hope of glory.

OPTIONAL EXTRA

Ask everyone to bring photos of family members that most of the group have not met. See if you can match up people with the photos of their family by spotting a family resemblance. Use this to set the scene. We are show the family likeness of our heavenly Father.

5 1 John 3 v 11-24
FAMILY TIES

THE BIG IDEA
True children of God love their brothers and sisters.

SUMMARY
In the opening half of chapter 3, John said that we show we are God's children by living in obedience to God. In the second half of the chapter, he says that we show we are God's children by loving our fellow brothers and sisters. We are bound by family ties.

John identifies two great privileges that belong to members of God's family:

- **confidence**—our love for other Christians is a sign we are part of God's family (v 19-20)

- **prayer**—our Father delights to respond to requests from His children (v 21-24)

GUIDANCE ON QUESTIONS
2. Look at v 10 and 12. The children of the devil are characterised by hate.

3. Cain's story reveals the true nature of hatred. Cain's hatred climaxed in murder. Even if we do not commit murder, hatred is murder in the heart (see v 15 and Matthew 5 v 21-24). The command to love is from the beginning (v 11; see also 2 v 7). But hatred also goes back to the first human family. Ever since the fall of Adam into sin, humanity has been divided into the children of the devil and the children of God.

4. Look at v 14. The children of God are characterised by love. We love one another in the Christian family.

5. Look at v 12-13. Abel's sacrifice was righteous because he loved God. Cain hated Abel because Abel was on God's side. It has been the same ever since. The children of the devil hate those who are the children of God.

- **What signs of this have you found in your own experience?**

6. The cross defines love. It is both the motive and benchmark of Christian love. True love is self-sacrificial. It is not based on sentiment, nor on the loveliness of the person to whom love is directed.

7. APPLY: People can talk about the lavish love of God without loving their brothers and sisters. People can talk about the church as a loving community without getting involved in other people's lives. Some people get excited by the 'idea' of love without ever getting stuck into serving other people. As someone said:
> To dwell above with saints in love,
>   that will indeed be glory;
> To dwell below with saints we know,
>   well, that's a different story!

8. APPLY:

- **What needs are there in your church community?**

9. Our hearts condemn us when we think of our sin. We worry about whether we are truly Christians.

10. 'This then' could refer back to the previous verses: we have confidence in God's presence because we love His family (see 3 v 14). Or it could refer forward: we have confidence in God's presence because God is greater than our hearts. Commentators are divided and John uses both arguments. God overcomes the restlessness of our hearts by powerfully reminding us, through His Spirit, that we are forgiven and that our condemnation has been taken by Christ on the cross (1 v 9 – 2 v 2).

11. If our hearts are at rest in God's presence, then we will not fear to come into His presence. If we are not condemned by God, then we can be confident before God in prayer. Having hearts that do not condemn us does not mean living a perfect life, but trusting that Christ has dealt with our condemnation.

12. Look at how John continues. God gives what we ask for when we pray for what pleases Him. And what pleases God is that we believe in His Son, Jesus, and that we love one another. God gives us what we ask when we pray for faith and love. He does this through the gift of the Spirit (v 24).

13. APPLY: We should pray confidently, because we trust that God will receive us because of Christ's work on our behalf. We should not pray because we are confident in our own goodness. We should pray for more faith and love.

• **Compare the things you normally pray for with the things John suggests we should pray for.**

OPTIONAL EXTRA

Come up with an idea for a way the group could show love for other Christians immediately in a practical way. It could be anything from collecting money for a believer in need or writing letters to Christians serving overseas, to baking cakes for struggling Christians in your church.

1 John 4 v 1-21
TRUE LOVE

THE BIG IDEA
The Spirit of God enables us to believe the truth about Jesus and love one another. As a result, we need not fear judgment because we can be confident we are God's children.

SUMMARY
John ends chapter 3 by talking about the reassurance the Spirit gives us (3 v 24). So in 4 v 1-6 he tells us how we can discern the true work of the Spirit. The work of God's Spirit is characterised by the belief that Jesus is truly God and truly human. Anything else is the work of the spirit of antichrist.

Through the Spirit we are born again of God and God is present in our lives. And so, in 4 v 7-12, John says this means we will live a life of love (see also v 20-21). John's argument is this: God is love. We are of God. Therefore we should love. And our love is modelled on the cross.

God wants us to be confident that we are His children (v 14-16), so that His love can achieve its goal: confidence on the day of judgment (v 17). God's love to us and our love for one another dispel the fear of judgment (v 18-19).

GUIDANCE ON QUESTIONS
2. Christians need to be discerning because not every spirit is of God. There are false teachers inspired by the spirit of antichrist. Compare 2 v 18-23 with 4 v 1-3.

3. The Holy Spirit glorifies Jesus (see John 16 v 13-15). So the Holy Spirit's work is characterised by the belief that Jesus is truly God and truly human. In John's context some people were denying that Jesus was truly human. They are, says John, not inspired by God's Spirit, but by the spirit of antichrist.

4. Look at verses 4-6. God is greater than the spirits that inspire false teaching. Even when the truth is attacked, we can be sure that we are on the winning side. False views are popular because they speak from a worldly viewpoint. Worldly people listen to them because they hear what they want to hear (see 2 Timothy 4 v 3).

5. APPLY: False spirituality is not a step to true spirituality, but a step away from it. The value of any 'spirituality' must be determined by its view of Jesus.

6. APPLY: It is important to manage the answers to this question in a responsible way. We have a tendency to be suspicious of anything that is 'different' from our own church experience. But there are (and should be!) many differences of personality and culture in the expression of Christian faith, both for individual believers, and for whole congregations. That said, there are very subtle ways that people will agree with the statement that 'Jesus Christ came in the flesh', and yet their practices and other beliefs undermine it.

There are many false claims about Jesus that say he is less than God ('Jesus minus'), and these are often easier to spot than the 'Jesus plus' claims, which agree that He is fully God and fully man, and yet insist that there is some other experience, ritual or knowledge that is needed in addition to Jesus. By adding to Jesus, people, in effect, take away from Him, because the implication is that He is not enough, and we need these extra things to bring us into the presence of God.

7. John's argument is this: God is love. We are of God. Therefore we should love.

8. We love because we are born of the God who is love. So our love should be like God's love. And the supreme

⌄
• **What does the cross reveal about God's love?** God's love is *costly* (He gave His only son). God's love is *undeserved* (He did not wait for us to love Him). God's love is effective or *practical* (He gives us life and atonement—the word translated 'atoning sacrifice' is *propitiation*. See the comments on 2 v 2 (p.11).

expression of God's love is the cross.
9. First, the Spirit testifies that we are Christians (v 13). Secondly, true Christians believe the truth about Jesus (v 14). This shows we are true Christians because acknowledging the truth is a sign of God at work in our lives (v 15). Thirdly, true Christians love one another because they are children of the God of love (v 16).

EXPLORE MORE

Some people suggest love is more

important than truth; others that truth is more important than love. But John defines love and truth in the same way: God sending His Son into the world to save us.

10. It is not clear whether John is talking in verse 17 about God's love to us or our love for one another. Since John connects them so tightly, it may be both. The goal of love is confidence on the day of judgment.

11. To fear God is to feel awe before His majesty, sovereignty, splendour and holiness. We should fear God in this way (eg: Proverbs 9 v 10). In verse 17 John is talking about the day of judgment. We do not fear God's judgment. Love gives us confidence that we are God's children.

12. God does not love us because we are lovely or loving. He loves us because He is love. His love for us is based on His character, not our character. So His love for us will not change if we change. Indeed He started loving us when we were His enemies.

13. APPLY: We display something of the gospel message through our relationships with one another in the Christian community (see John 13 v 34-35 and 17 v 23). We attract people to the Christian message by reflecting something of God's character. When, for example, Christians doubt God's goodness or control, we can remind them of God's love through our actions, as well as our words.

1 John 5 v 1-21
TRUE CONFIDENCE

THE BIG IDEA

Christians can and should have confidence in the truth, in the future and in prayer.

SUMMARY

John returns to most of the themes he has developed in his letter. He is like someone holding a diamond up to the light. The same truths are seen from different angles so that we can catch their beauty. Moreover, John increasingly weaves all his themes together to show how they inter-relate.

John writes this letter so that we might have confidence as Christians (v 13).

In v 1-5 John shows how faith, rebirth, love and obedience mutually reinforce one another to give us victory over the world.

In v 6-12 John shows that we can have confidence in the truth about Jesus because of the testimony of the apostles and God Himself. This confidence in the truth leads to confident hope for eternal life.

In v 14-17 John shows that confidence that we are God's children leads to confidence in prayer.

In v 18-20 John shows that we can have confidence for the future. Our assurance is secure because God will keep us in the face of a hostile and deceitful world.

John ends with a call to keep ourselves from idols (v 21). We should not compromise the confidence we can have as Christians by continuing to sin.

GUIDANCE ON QUESTIONS

2. Faith ➤ rebirth ➤ love ➤ obedience. And all of them together lead to victory. Faith, love and obedience mutually reinforce one another in our lives. Faith and practice go together. To trust God is to love God, and to love God is to obey God.

3. See 2 v 15-17. The world encourages us to disobey God by following our sinful cravings and lusts. We overcome the world by loving and obeying God.

4. The Spirit testifies that Jesus is divine. This may be a reference to the Spirit descending on Jesus at His baptism—see John 1 v 32-34. Or it may refer to the Spirit's testimony in our hearts (see 4 v 13-14 and 5 v 10). **The water** may be a reference to the voice of the Father at the baptism of Jesus (Mark 1 v 9-11). **The blood**—the false teachers may have said Jesus was not God on the cross because God could not die. But John says the cross shows Jesus *is* God, because only God would show such amazing love (4 v 9-10). In a Jewish court, evidence had to be corroborated by two or three witnesses (Deuteronomy 19 v 15). John has produced three witnesses.

5. See 1 v 1-4. Man's testimony to Jesus is the experience of the apostles, including John himself.

6. God's testimony is the sum of the three witnesses: Spirit, water and blood. The apostles saw and heard Jesus and concluded that He was divine (man's testimony). It was human judgement (albeit one made with the help of the Spirit). How much stronger is God's judgement. God should be able to recognise Himself!

7. People sometimes say theology does not matter (love matters more), or that theology is boring, or that theology is deadening. Look at verse 10. To diminish Jesus is to call God a liar. Look at v 11-12. The testimony of God about His Son leads to eternal life. What is at stake with theology is our salvation. If we do not believe the truth about Jesus, then we do not have life.

8.
- Do you believe in Jesus? (4 v 15; 5 v 1)
- Do you love other Christians? (2 v 10; 3 v 10, 14, 18-19)
- Do you want to obey God's commands? (2 v 3 - 6)
- Do you know the testimony of the Spirit? (3 v 24; 4 v 13)

These signs are not a checklist, but inter-related confirmations.

9. The Bible talks about the will of God in two ways. It talks about His sovereign will which determines all events. This is secret. We cannot normally know it ahead of time. The Bible also talks about God's moral will = the way He wants people to live. God reveals this in the Bible (the Word of God) and in Jesus (the Word of God). Praying according to God's will is not second-guessing God's sovereign will. It is praying in accordance with God's revealed will. It is asking for those things which God desires or has promised to give.

EXPLORE MORE
In the light of 1 v 3, we can pray that we might have fellowship with God through faith in Jesus. In the light of 1 v 9, we can pray that God would forgive specific sins.

10. God's will is that believers should be holy. God's will is that believers should repent of sin and find life in Jesus. So to pray in accordance with God's will for fallen believers is to pray for their restoration. John talks about a sin that leads to death. He is probably talking about apostasy—confessing faith in Christ and then turning away from Him (2 v 18-19). The sin of believers does not lead to death because Christ has died for us (1 v 9 –2 v 2). But we cannot pray that the sin of those who turn from Christ will be forgiven because they no longer have saving faith in Christ.

• **What do we actually do when we see other believers sinning?**
Often our tendency is to gossip.

11. First, we know God will keep us (v 18). We may have assurance of salvation now (v 13), but will it last? Jesus will keep us safe from the evil one. Secondly, we know we belong to God (v 19). The whole world might be against us, but that is because it belongs to the evil one, while we belong to God. Thirdly, we know what we know is true (v 20). The world is full of false claims, but we know the One who is the truth—Jesus Christ.

12. In a hostile world we can keep going as Christians, confident that God will keep us because we are His. In a deceitful world we can keep believing as Christians, confident that Jesus gives us an understanding of the truth. We will not continue to sin because we are born of the holy God (v 18).

13. Idolatry is the root cause of all sin. We put other things before God.
We desire them more than we desire God. They may be good things, but they become more important to us than God. Idolatry causes sinful behaviour and sinful behaviour undermines our confidence. John writes his letter to give us confidence. He does not want us undermining that confidence.

OPTIONAL EXTRA

This Good Book Guide is called *How to be sure*. Have a general discussion with the group about the areas of 'being sure' it has covered. Get the group to talk about before... and after. Eg: 'Before I started this study, I was not confident I was a Christian, but now I am sure that I belong to Him.' Make sure that people express what it is in John's letter that has helped them to grow in confidence.